DREAM JOBS IN SPORTS SCOUTING

MARTY GITLIN

ROSEN
PUBLISHING®

New York

Published in 2015 by The Rosen Publishing Group, Inc.
29 East 21st Street, New York, NY 10010

Copyright © 2015 by The Rosen Publishing Group, Inc.

First Edition

Library of Congress Cataloging-in-Publication Data

Gitlin, Marty.
Dream jobs in sports scouting / Marty Gitlin.
    pages cm.—(Great careers in the sports industry)
Includes bibliographical references and index.
ISBN 978-1-4777-7518-9 (library bound)
1. Sports agents. 2. Sports—Vocational guidance. I. Title.
GV734.5.G52 2014
796.06'9—dc23

                                                    2013038935

Manufactured in the United States of America

CONTENTS

INTRODUCTION

Baseball scouts are seen here at a major league exhibition game in Florida using radar guns, which measure the speed of base runners and various pitches thrown by pitchers.

It was the summer of 1935. Cleveland Indians scout Cy Slapnicka was traveling to Iowa farm country. He intended to assess a pitcher named Claude Passeau, who was pitching for Des Moines in the Western League.

But Slapnicka never saw the kid toss one ball to the plate. When he arrived, an umpire tipped him off about a seventeen-year-old boy named Bob Feller from a tiny town called Van Meter. Slapnicka sat on a car bumper and watched in awe as Feller fired blazing fastballs that wiggled and darted before thumping into the catcher's mitt. Hapless batters flailed away in vain.

"I knew I was looking at an arm the likes of which you see only once in a lifetime," Slapnicka later said, according to Russell Schneider's *The Cleveland Indians Encyclopedia*. He raved about Feller in a meeting of Indians directors. "Gentlemen, I've found the greatest young pitcher I ever saw," he told them. "I suppose this sounds like the same old stuff, but this boy will be one of the greatest pitchers the world has ever known."

In the modern era, every scout in baseball would have known about Feller, even though he had yet to hurl a pitch as a high school junior. He likely would have been taken with the first pick of the major league draft and received a multimillion-dollar bonus.

But this was 1935. There was no draft. Slapnicka kept his cool. He did not reveal to Feller his belief that he was destined for stardom. He was the only major league scout who had seen him pitch. So he signed Feller for $1 and an autographed baseball!

The rest is history. Feller pitched his first game with the Indians at age seventeen and indeed emerged as one of the finest pitchers in the history of the sport. And though Slapnicka was responsible for signing many star players, his name will forever be linked with Feller.

Times have changed drastically. Scouts from every National Football League (NFL) and National Basketball Association (NBA) franchise are keenly aware of all the top college players in their sports. Major League Baseball (MLB) and National Hockey League (NHL) scouts know all about the premier high school and college prospects. They still travel to the remote regions of the United States and throughout the world to analyze every athlete with the potential to perform at the highest levels. There are no secrets anymore.

Yet that universal awareness of the premier athletes heightens the challenge for every scout. The huge contracts offered to athletes recommended by scouts to be drafted, or signed as free agents, make it imperative that such endorsements are warranted. Scouts who are consistently wrong in their assessments do not remain in their jobs for long.

Despite the pressure placed upon scouts, they are perhaps the most underappreciated professionals in the world of sports. Their names remain unknown to the public and generally unmentioned by the sports media. But they are among the most important employees to their respective teams. Their insight and evaluation of athletes is critical to the success of a sports franchise. Front offices are dependent on their scouts to play a most important role in player procurement.

Those who scour the nation and even the world for talent for big-league franchises do not make up the entire sports scouting business. Several areas of scouting must be understood by anyone contemplating a career in that field.

Chapter 1

LITTLE VARIETY, PLENTY OF PRESSURE

The sports world is not exactly teeming with many different types of scouts. There are high school and college scouts that find and judge talent. There are professional scouts who assess players on rival teams for possible trades or free agent signings. There are advance scouts who evaluate players from other organizations and report back to their coaches about how best to attack or defend them in upcoming games.

Simple, right? Not really. The life and work of any of those scouts is far more complex. Homebodies need not apply. A scouting career requires a willingness to travel most of the year. The job necessitates a keen eye for talent and a strong knowledge of the intricacies of an athlete's strengths and weaknesses. It entails not just hundreds of hours watching prospects in live action but thousands of hours evaluating them on tape. It is not enough to recommend a hitter because he boasts a lot of power or a quarterback for his strong arm. A scout must assess in detail every physical, mental, and emotional side of an athlete.

After all, the core of the job description for high school and college scouts is to calculate the productivity of an athlete at the highest professional level. It is part science and part speculation. Every scout must live with failure. They sometimes recommend to their organizations that they reject a player who later blossoms into a star. They sometimes endorse an athlete who flops after he is drafted or signed. But the most successful scouts use their experience and knowledge to evaluate correctly most of the talent with whom their eyes come in contact. Scouts can only hope they are right in their predictions more often than not.

High school scouting is particularly speculative. Projecting the contribution of a prep baseball player in the major leagues or hockey player in the NHL is difficult. Obvious talents such as three-time NBA Most Valuable Player LeBron James, who was drafted out of high school before the league banned the drafting of prep players, come around once in a generation. It is far easier to predict the performances of major college athletes, who are further developed mentally, emotionally, and physically, and have already competed against a higher level of competition. That is why NFL scouts boast an advantage. They evaluate just college talent because teams can draft or sign only players who have competed in at least three years of

The annual draft connects amateur players with NHL franchises. Calgary Flames scout Ron Sutter is shown here greeting draft pick Jon Gillies in June 2012.

college football. There is no need for them to scout high school talent. The NBA requires merely one year of college experience.

But despite their awareness of the speculative nature of their business, scouts must remain strong in their convictions. They must exude enough confidence to believe in themselves and their ability to evaluate talent effectively. Among those who have achieved success in the business is Dan Shonka, who serves as general manager and national scout for the Ourlads Scouting Service, which has been providing NFL teams draft guides and reports about college talent for more than three decades. In an interview with the author, Shonka listed a number of personality and attitude traits necessary to thrive as a scout.

"You must have persistence and enthusiasm and you must be goal-oriented and self-confident," Shonka said. "You have to believe in your abilities. It also takes discipline, commitment, trustworthiness, responsibility, decisiveness, hard work, intelligence, organization, self-sacrifice and sincerity. You also have to be articulate with the courage to state and support your beliefs about a player."

Those qualities are essential for all scouts. But although conviction is important and scouts should not be swayed by opposing views, they also must keep an open mind. Those who offer a differing opinion about a prospect could very well boast sound points. The best scouts find it wise to explore the validity of negative or positive comments about a player that contradicts their own to confirm they are being thorough in the evaluations they provide their organizations.

DIFFERENT SCOUTS FOR DIFFERENT JOBS

The word "scout" implies a job working with a professional sports organization or service. Every NBA, NHL, NFL, and MLB franchise boasts an extensive scouting department that supplies vast information about prospects

BLAZING A PATH FOR WOMEN

Edith Houghton was thirty-three years old when she worked up the courage to walk into the office of Philadelphia Phillies president Robert Carpenter and ask for a job as a scout. She told Carpenter he had nothing to lose—after all, his team was a perennial loser in the National League.

It was 1946. Houghton knew her baseball. She had played the sport in the 1920s and 1930s in a women's national circuit called the Bloomer Girls League. Soon she had convinced Carpenter to hire her as the first and only female MLB scout. In an interview that year with the *Sporting News*, she explained her criteria for evaluating players.

"First of all, I shall look for size," she said. "Players must be big, and they must be fast. But they must be able to hit. I learned early in my baseball career that you can't steal first base."

Houghton has remained the only female scout in the history of MLB. But Frank Marcos, who served as senior director of the MLB Scouting Bureau, would like to add more to the list.

"We know of no other part-time or full-time woman scouts in baseball since then," he reported. "Would I like to change that? Darn right."

Houghton was not, however, the only female scout in the history of major American sports. In 2006, fifty-eight years after the Phillies hired Houghton, a young woman named Bonnie-Jill Laflin secured a scouting job with the NBA Los Angeles Lakers.

Laflin took quite a different route to her job. She had toiled as an NFL and NBA cheerleader and sports broadcaster before Lakers owner Jerry Buss, who had specifically set out to find a qualified woman for that position, hired her as a scout.

across America and, in leagues that feature vast numbers of foreign players, throughout the world.

But scouting has not always been done by scouts. College programs have sent assistant coaches and even head coaches to scout and recruit high school talent for possible scholarships and sometimes to watch games played by upcoming opponents to begin the process of preparing for them. In August 2013, the National Collegiate Athletic Association (NCAA) launched a ban of live scouting of opponents with the thought that limiting teams to video analysis would even the playing field. But high school sports programs also dispatch assistant coaches to scout future foes. The job description of many college and high school coaches includes scouting. Their work often proves invaluable to their teams.

In fact, recruiting is a form of scouting that can make or break a college athletics program. Coaches must not only project the physical talent of high school athletes to the next level but also determine whether they are worthy of a scholarship. They must judge emotional and mental strength through academic performance, behavioral patterns, background, and many other factors. Though they are not scouts by profession, their job requirements are quite similar to those at the professional sports level who do hold that title.

Personal interaction is critical to the evaluation of high school and college players. It is particularly important when

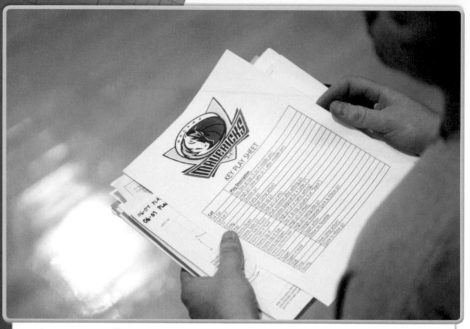

A Phoenix Suns staff member reviews the scouting report for a Dallas Mavericks player during a team practice. Professional scouts evaluate players on rival teams for possible trades or free agent signings and advance scouts assess opposing team players and report back to their coaches about how best to attack or defend them in future games.

scouting and recruiting at the prep level to meet and impress not only athletes but their families as well. Strong positive feelings must be mutual on both sides for the relationships between scouts, families, and athletes to reach a successful conclusion. Family considerations often prove less critical to college prospects, most of whom have gained a sense of independence of thought. Though college athletes have little say in their immediate futures—their employment is most often determined by the draft—they must also exude the strength of character and passion for their sport that scouts or coaches seek in high school athletes. During his interview with the author, Shonka expressed those sentiments and grew more specific in his assessment of what a scout looks for in an amateur athlete.

"Outside the obvious physical characteristics, you must know if the athlete has leadership ability," Shonka explained. "Was he a team captain? Is he coachable? How quickly does he learn? Does he have an injury history or durability problems? Has he been arrested or suspended? Who has had the most influence on his career? Is he self-motivated? How is he best motivated? How does he respond to praise and criticism? These are all important considerations.

"You also want to know his football intelligence. How does he learn the best? Can he carry what he learns on the [chalkboard] onto the football field? Does he learn best on the computer, tape, walk-throughs, or full-speed reps on the field? If he didn't play football, what would he do in life? Scouts have to ask all of these questions."

Another prominent function of a scout at the professional level can be the evaluation of a player in anticipation of a possible trade. The practice is particularly common in baseball, where such swaps are often completed. Scouts are often sent to assess the strengths and weaknesses of players being considered for acquisition. Past performance motivates possible trades. Scouts, however, must project future production. Scouts in attendance at major league or minor league games are generally there to check out a player in which his team has expressed interest. The sports media has increased their coverage of such scouts in recent years as they report on possible deals between teams not only in MLB but also in the NBA and NHL.

SCOUTING FOR A SHOWDOWN

Advance scouts never consider the questions asked by scouts of high school and college players. Their responsibilities are quite different—though advance scouting is an integral part of the prep and college sports worlds as well.

High school and college scouts assess players to determine their worthiness of competing at the next level. Advance scouts are dispatched by their teams or organizations to watch a future foe in game action. They are generally sent to report not on one individual but rather an entire team. Their mission is to give their coaches, managers, and players the most complete analysis so that they can put together the best plan to defeat that opponent.

Scouts are often seen at spring exhibition games like this matchup between the Oakland Athletics and Cleveland Indians at Municipal Stadium in Phoenix, Arizona.

In an interview with the author, St. Louis Cardinals baseball scout Michael Juhl clarified the differences between amateur scouting and advance scouting in his sport. "Scouting amateur players is done in preparation for the draft that takes place each year in early June," he explained. "Advance scouting is done to help the major league team in knowing its opponent's strengths, weaknesses, and tendencies. An advance scout is usually one or two series' ahead of the club and provides an in-depth report a day or two in advance of the games."

The schedules are a bit different for advance scouts in the NFL, NBA, and NHL, but their missions are the same. Their importance cannot be understated in regard to preparing their teams for battles ahead. The modern era of sports has become overwhelmed with statistical analysis. There is certainly value in such numbers. But the increased depth in that area will never replace the worth of an experienced scout soaking in live game action and providing his coaches and players with information that best prepares them to defend and attack opponents.

Advance scouting has been universal in all levels of sports for generations. The only variance at the top professional levels is the job title of scout. Head coaches and their assistants, particularly in such "major" high school and college sports as football and basketball, are also dispatched regularly to games played by future opponents to gather information. They are simply coaches whose job responsibilities include scouting.

Top college football players often schedule a "Pro Day" to give NFL scouts a chance to evaluate their skills. Shown here is quarterback Terrelle Pryor displaying his talent in August 2011.

Not all scouting is done firsthand. High school and college athletes often send taped highlights of game action to impress college and pro scouts, as well as video coordinators, who spend hundreds of hours poring over them.

The job is difficult. After all, athletes tend to show themselves only at their best. Baseball batters send tapes of their longest home runs, pitchers their nastiest curveballs. Football running backs show their sweetest moves, defensive backs their most impressive interceptions. Basketball point guards show their quickest slashes to the basket, centers their finest blocked shots. Those who watch them on film must project their contributions against a higher level of athletic competition without a firsthand view. Coaches and scouts then pick the most intriguing to see live at both their best and worst. It is only then that they can make a thorough analysis of the athletes' physical talents. Those whom scouts feel boast the greatest athletic skills are then evaluated to decide if they also have the determination, intensity, intelligence, and other attributes to succeed at a high level of competition.

Player evaluation, however, is an inexact science. Scouts measure every specific physical and emotional attribute and failing of every athlete he sees. A football scout will measure how quickly a quarterback releases the ball. A baseball scout will clock a base runner sprinting from second base to home plate on a single. A basketball scout will determine how high a forward jumps to grab a rebound. They will talk to coaches and even parents to gain an understanding of the mental and emotional strengths and weaknesses of a particular athlete. Yet the scouts' gauging of players' abilities still fall under the category of speculation.

Many athletes touted by scouts as a future superstar have failed to earn one moment of playing time in the big leagues. Other athletes whom scouts have claimed to be lacking in talent have blossomed into all-time greats. The NFL New England Patriots did not select quarterback Tom

New England Patriots quarterback Tom Brady, shown here against the Cleveland Browns in 2001, blossomed into a superstar after being taken in the sixth round of the 2000 draft.

Brady until the 199th pick of the 2000 draft. Yet he led his team to three Super Bowl championships and is considered one of the greatest quarterbacks in football history.

Scouts must also contend with fellow scouts and general managers who do not take their advice. One such example revolved around veteran Philadelphia Phillies scout Brandy Davis. Davis was sent to Florida in the spring of 1980 to scout highly touted high school catcher Henry Powell. Another Phillies scout compared Powell to Hall of Fame slugger Jimmie Foxx. But Davis gave quite a different assessment after watching Powell play. His story, which shows the detail in which scouts assess prospects, was related in a book titled *Dollar Sign on the Muscle: The World of Baseball Scouting.* "I stopped in Pensacola that April and [Powell] looked so far from what they told me about, just to be fair, I stayed over an extra day to watch him in another game," Davis said. "In all I saw him take two long batting practices and another six times in games. He was a high-ball hitter, but not with a home run swing—he one-handed the bat. On low pitches he chopped at the ball. His swing didn't coordinate his hips and legs. As a catcher he showed … poor instincts, bad hands. His throws to second weren't accurate, and they were all shoulder: no strong forearm or wrist action. So after that second game I red-carded him—'No prospect.'"

The Phillies ignored the evaluation. They chose Powell in the first round of the draft that spring. He played three years in the lower minor leagues and never batted over .248. He was out of baseball by 1983.

Scouts in all sports experience failure. Even when they are right about a player, their evaluations are sometimes overlooked by those that make decisions on player procurement. But though they rarely receive credit for their successes from fans and the sports media, they are greatly appreciated by their organizations and their jobs are generally exciting and rewarding. Those who believe they might embrace such a profession can begin preparing for it in high school or even earlier.

Chapter 2

SO YOU WANT TO BE A SCOUT?

First things first—high school students should not commit to pursue a career as a scout until they understand the lifestyle demanded of those in the field. Most important, they must know that if they enjoy quiet evenings at home with their families, they should try another profession.

Just ask Greg Gabriel. He has spent more than three decades as a scout with the NFL New York Giants, Buffalo Bills, Chicago Bears, and Philadelphia Eagles. He wrote an article for the *National Football Post* in 2010, during his tenure as director of college scouting with the Bears, that detailed the tremendous amount of travel required in his job. If those considering a career in scouting are not deterred by his explanation, they are certainly qualified to pursue that line of work. Gabriel explained that scouts must be self-motivated and independent thinkers. They must also boast outstanding time management skills

Minor league baseball and basketball teams often use assistant coaches as advance scouts. Idaho Stampede assistant coach Ray Lopes is seen here scouting the Fort Wayne Flyers.

because the amount of work on their plates is often more than what can be handled in a typical day. Gabriel added the following about scouts in his piece:

> *They spend an inordinate amount of time on the road away from their families. Over the last 26 years, there were many times that I spent well over 200 nights a year on the road. Because of the dedication you have to have for your job, you end up missing a lot at home. You miss some of your kids' sporting events or school plays. You might miss your baby's first steps. I missed the birth of my first child because I couldn't get home fast enough to be there.*

Those who believe they can feel comfortable with the amount of travel involved in scouting can then start attaining the skills to build a foundation for a career. It is never too early to begin by observing and evaluating athletes in sports in which scouts are utilized, such as baseball, football, basketball, hockey, and soccer. These steps can be achieved not only by witnessing the performances of individual players on their high school or local college teams live but also through taking a more studious approach to watching games on television. Though those contemplating a career in scouting might feel a greater sense of passion for one particular sport, it is wise for them to hone their skills by assessing players in as many sports as can be realistically seen in person and on television.

High school students can take several practical steps toward gaining experience in the art of scouting. Among them is to observe and jot down notes about the perceived strengths and weaknesses about a player in game action. Study his or her general athletic skills, such as speed, quickness, strength, and leaping ability. Examine the player's sport-specific talents, such as bat speed for a baseball player, footwork while blocking for an offensive lineman in football, ability to box out while rebounding in basketball, or puck management for a forward in hockey. Then rate the amount of passion and intensity the player exudes for his or her sport. If the athlete you are scouting is a friend or fellow high school student you know, consider factors such as academic performance, motivation, emotional stability, and intelligence and decide if such off-the-field considerations would prove to be a positive or negative influence on his or her college or professional potential.

Keep in mind also that your high school coaches can prove beneficial to those starting on the path to a scouting career. It would be wise to inform your head or assistant coaches of such an intention. Ask their permission to provide a detailed scouting report of one of their players. Their examination of your analysis will result in advice and insight that could make you a better scout. Do not stop at the sport for which you boast the most knowledge and passion. Scout athletes in all sports in which the profession is prominent.

TAKING IT OFF CAMPUS

Your foray into scouting can extend beyond the athletes at your school. Inquire if you can accompany a high school coach on a scouting mission at a sporting event involving an upcoming opponent. The practice is done most often in football and basketball, but head coaches and assistant coaches in other sports also travel to learn more about a future foe. That will give you an opportunity to focus not only on the potential of individual players but also on team tendencies, strengths, and weaknesses. It will allow

Prospective scouts are often taught the tools of the trade outside college settings. NFL scout Russ Lande is shown here giving advice to students for Sports Management Worldwide.

you to gain the experience of an advance scout. Observe your coaches as they evaluate the opposition. Inquire how their assessment will allow their team to exploit their upcoming opponent on the field or court.

Most high school sports teams do not utilize coaches as advance scouts. That could provide an opportunity for those considering a scouting career to learn the trade through personal involvement. One should not be too shy to ask coaches if they intend to scout games involving a future competitor. Perhaps coaches in various sports will allow you to become their official scout. Never mind if it is in a sport that does not use scouts at the college or professional levels. The experience of assessing athletes' strengths and weaknesses, as well as team tendencies, would prove invaluable and look impressive on a résumé when the time comes to seek an internship or spot in a scouting school.

There is no better person to learn scouting from than a scout. They are not hard to find at a high school sporting event. They are holding stopwatches to measure the speed of a football player, a radar gun to time the fastball of a pitcher, or a clipboard to write an evaluation of a prep basketball star. They are wherever a premier athlete can be found. Sometimes there are many scouts gathered to assess the talent of a top prospect, particularly in events with high levels of competition.

TO PLAY OR NOT TO PLAY? THAT IS THE QUESTION

Parents have been complaining in recent years that the kids of the modern generation are not active enough. But when it comes to high school sports, they're more active than they have been in decades.

A survey released by the National Federation of State High School Associations (NFHS) in September 2011 revealed that the number of students participating in at least one sport had risen for twenty-two consecutive years. More than 7.6 million high school students had participated during the 2010–2011 school year. That was an increase of about 40,000 from the previous season.

"It's amazing that participation has increased for 22 consecutive years," says John Gillis, associate director of publications and communications at NFHS. "Nowadays, there are so many diversions and distractions for students. I think sports are so popular because they give students the opportunity to be a part of something. There's camaraderie on these teams."

The most common sport that school year was basketball. A total of 18,150 schools boasted a boys' basketball team and 17,767 schools had a girls' team. But football was being played by more students than any other sport. More than 1.1 million students had participated in football in about 14,000 schools.

The fastest growing sport, however, was girls' lacrosse, where participation jumped by 6,155 students from the 2009–2010 school year. In fact, girls' sports in general had experienced quite a leap. Girls made up 41 percent of all high school athletes, which represented a

5 percent rise from 1991. Considering virtually no girls play football, that is a telling statistic.

Despite the time and effort required of athletes, studies have also shown that those who participate in sports are slightly better students. As reported by Jason Koebler in *U.S. News*, a 2007 survey of high schools in Minnesota revealed that student athletes boasted a mean grade point average of 2.84 compared to 2.68 for nonathletes.

It is both wise and empowering to sidle up to one of them and strike up a conversation. Let the scout know that you are planning to follow the same career path. As long as you are not interfering with their work, most scouts will be flattered that you are intrigued by their profession and will be glad to offer advice. They might also allow you to watch them in action as they scout the athlete or athletes they have come to evaluate. High school students should come prepared to take full advantage of such an opportunity by writing out questions beforehand about the lifestyle of a scout as well as what he looks for in a player in that particular sport. Most scouts will also be willing to share information about the best way to get into the business. Those fortunate enough might find a scout who will remain a contact or even a reference after the student graduates high school or college and begins seeking internships or jobs with professional franchises.

TWO POINTS OF VIEW

When it comes to prospective scouts attending high school, there are two ways of thinking. One is that it is not necessary to participate in sports. That philosophy is based on the belief that one can learn about the field more from observing than playing. One might feel that athletes are too busy concentrating on honing their own talents to judge those of others.

Those who claim that students can play a role on a team as a nonathlete bolster the validity of that view. Prospective scouts might volunteer their services, for instance, as an equipment manager, to stay close to the team and earn the opportunity to watch games from the sideline, where scouting skills can be groomed. Not everyone can play a major sport in high school and those who cannot should not be dissuaded from pursuing a career in scouting.

Many scouts, however, hold the opposite view. They would not go so far as to claim that nonparticipation as an athlete precludes the possibility of eventually landing a job

These student equipment managers at the University of South Carolina prepare some of the footballs and helmets for an upcoming game. Volunteering as an equipment manager enables a prospective scout to pick up some valuable knowledge.

in scouting. But they offer that playing sports, especially those whose participants are scouted at the high school, college, and professional levels, can prove advantageous because it provides an appreciation of the athleticism necessary to excel. They further contend that playing a sport also gives one a better understanding of the game itself.

In an interview with the author, Ourlads Scouting Service and national scout Dan Shonka stated that he falls squarely in the latter camp, at least concerning football. He considers participation a preferable option, though not a necessity. He stated in an interview with the author that the sport should border on an obsession for students who seek a scouting career in football.

"A student who wants to scout must eat, drink, and sleep football," Shonka said. "You must have a fire in your [belly] to be willing to work 14–16 hours a day because you enjoy being a scout and nothing else is more important in your life. Playing high school football, whether you are a star or scout team player, helps you understand the techniques and fundamentals of the game. The special abilities that are acquired through playing football, training, and first-hand experience cannot be underestimated."

Shonka believes that high school students can best learn the intricacies of football that are required knowledge for scouts by playing the game. The same can be argued for other sports in which scouting plays a role, such as baseball, basketball, hockey, and soccer. It is one thing to watch from the sideline or in the stands and judge the overall athleticism of a player or the tendencies of a team in one of those sports. It is quite another to evaluate the sport-specific skills of an individual without having experienced competing in that sport. This is not to claim that participation in a particular sport is a prerequisite to forging a career in scouting in that sport. A passion for scouting and willingness to learn and practice can translate into success. But familiarity with the physical and mental complexities of the sport through playing certainly helps.

So does practical experience. That can be achieved not only at the high school level through informal scouting of athletes in action but also through scouting schools and online courses that prepare young people for the profession. What must be remembered, however, is that most full-time sports scouts have gained experience through playing or coaching at the high school, college, or even professional level. A high school education and a bit of scouting practice at games do not qualify one to launch a career in the business. One must boast experience that is far more practical. For instance, the MLB Scouting Development Program requires a recommendation from a major league team for a student to gain acceptance. That recommendation is generally earned through relevant work in college and beyond.

Chapter 3

STUDYING SPORTS, WORKING TOWARD A CAREER

O ne of the keys to life is patience. Those seeking a career in scouting should eventually target the sport in which they yearn to work, become heavily involved with the sports teams or athletics department in college, study hard, and earn a relevant degree. Professional scouts most often come from the ranks of players and coaches, but there are other avenues. Those who have shown the commitment to finish college while working toward a vocation impress organizations that hire scouts. Those who hurriedly seek to forge a scouting career without a college education are destined for disappointment.

The importance of a college education and securing a degree extends far beyond training for one particular profession. The experience builds character, promotes strong study habits and work ethic, greatly increases a knowledge base in a wide variety of subjects, and adds social skills that prove invaluable in just about any line of work. Only

Scouting experts working for Sports Management Worldwide lend their knowledge and experience to teach prospective scouts about the business in sports such as baseball, football, basketball, and hockey.

those who are open to growing and embrace the college life can take full advantage of its benefits.

This is not to suggest that those yearning to become a scout should temporarily extinguish that flame. Though one cannot major specifically in scouting, hundreds of universities throughout the United States offer undergraduate and postgraduate degrees in sports management and sports administration. Both provide an overall understanding of the sports business, which has become far more complex in recent decades. Sports franchises or scouting services are far more likely to accept college graduates for scouting internships or scouting jobs.

They are also far more likely to hire those with practical experience—and college provides many such opportunities. Those who have offered their services to coaches as volunteer scouts in high school can further hone their skills by doing the same at the college level. One cannot be too shy to approach a coach in a sport that uses scouts, such as baseball, football, basketball, hockey, or soccer. In most cases at major universities, coaches are dispatched as advance scouts to assess the tendencies of future opponents. Feel free to ask if you can accompany them on a trip. Though the coaches might not utilize your growing expertise, you can learn about what they are looking for in preparing their team to face that foe. College coaches analyzing opponents on video see them from a different perspective than do their high school counterparts.

College coaches also undertake a job that high school coaches do not. That is, scouting and recruiting high school players. Though college students would likely not be given permission to accompany coaches on such missions to various parts of the country, those considering a scouting career should use them as a source of learning. Head coaches and assistant coaches, particularly those at the major college level, are vast resources of knowledge about scouting. Most would be glad to share that knowledge with students thirsting for it.

Perhaps the most important reason for prospective scouts to befriend college coaches is that professional sports organizations often hire scouts from the coaching ranks. It would be wise for any student eyeing such a career not only to take an interest in learning about the jobs and lifestyle of college coaches but also to strongly consider volunteering to help a coaching staff in any way deemed appropriate. That could lead to a job as a graduate assistant on a coaching staff. A college student seeking a career in scouting could decide that the best way to fulfill that desire is as a college coach that doubles as a scout and recruiter. Those who become established in that field are also better suited to gain employment at the highest level of professional sports.

ANOTHER ROAD FOR SCOUTS

Though steps can be taken toward a scouting career in college, the path is quite different from that of students seeking work in other professions. Because most scouts are hired from the ranks of players and coaches, the most important consideration is merely to earn a degree. And though earning that degree in sports management or sports administration can prove alluring to professional franchises seeking scouts, they are most impressed by those who have simply taken their college educations seriously enough to maximizing them. In an interview with the author, Ourlads Scouting Service general manager Don Shonka emphasized the need for prospective scouts to graduate.

"Majors such as physical education, journalism, speech, and sports management are desirable, but any major can work," he said. "A majority of NFL scouts have a coaching background. A college degree is important because it demonstrates your commitment to a goal. In a competitive world, earning an undergraduate degree puts you in the top 30 percent of the U.S. population. A master's degree boosts you to the top 7 percent of educated Americans.

"Working toward a degree, you meet others experiencing college life. A scout must be perceptive and observant. The college life will help you network for future jobs and craft more opportunities, enhancing your writing skills. College exposes you to many campus activities, as well as a variety of study, sports, and extracurricular programs. A degree in college builds your confidence. The bottom line is with our competitive and knowledge-based job market, the more pelts you have on your belt, the better."

The reference to writing talent is particularly applicable to scouting. High school and college scouts

A physical education student uses only his arms to climb a ropes course on campus. A major in physical education is frequently one that scouts have as their background, but earning any degree shows that a person is committed and can achieve goals.

Major League Baseball is the only league that boasts its own scouting school. The classroom is the baseball field, such as the Chicago Cubs minor league complex shown here in Mesa, Arizona.

must fill out extensive evaluations of the athletic skills as well as personal impressions of prospects. Advance scouts are required to do the same in assessing the strengths, weaknesses, and tendencies of upcoming opponents. The ability to write thoughtfully and clearly is an important component to the job of any scout. There can be no communication gap between a scout and his employer. The need is critical for those offering college scholarships to athletes and professional sports franchises signing players to multimillion-dollar contracts to thoroughly understand a scout's assessments.

The social aspect of college life is also important to those considering a scouting career. That is especially true for college coaches in their recruiting visits to high schools throughout the country. Those attempting to convince the finest prep athletes to accept a scholarship to their schools often must compete against scouts from hundreds of other major college programs. They must communicate to the coaches, players, and even their families that their school will not only provide the best outlet for athletic success but also maximize academic and social potential. A college choice is a life-changing decision. Convincing athletes to play sports at their schools requires a wide range of social and communication skills. Recruiters must be outgoing, friendly, honest, and understanding. The college experience provides potential scouts with the ability to learn the social amenities necessary to make successful forays into the world of recruiting.

The need for those same social skills is not as heightened in professional sports simply because there is less interaction with athletes. The most important talent for professional scouts is keen evaluation of college players or other teams. Most scouts at that level are not required to convince athletes to play in their organizations because the draft in MLB and the NHL determine the immediate fate of premier high school and college athletes. The NFL and NBA draft only college players and do not scout at the high school levels.

There are social aspects to any job, however, and professional scouts must be aware that they are one of the faces of their organizations. Though the draft makes it unnecessary for them to persuade college players to sign with their teams, they must use their social skills to learn enough about those players to recommend them to their teams preparing for the draft. That means interacting with coaches, trainers, and associates to confirm that those players boast the physical, mental, and emotional requirements to thrive at the top level of their sport. Long-time NFL scout Greg Gabriel understands that as well as anyone, as he explained in the following passage of an article he wrote for the *National Football Post*.

> *Good scouts need to spend many days during the course of the season at their key schools. They need to develop strong relationships with the key people that can help them with their evaluations. Many of these key people are not on the coaching or training staff, but rather support people [such as] academic advisors, secretaries, maintenance staff, who come in contact with the players on a daily basis. It is these people that really know the player. You need to know as much about the player off the field as you do on the field.*

This awareness is needed because the mental and emotional strengths and weaknesses of a prospect can often be just as important as those in the physical realm. It is the job of a scout to know through personal interaction and

FROM VIDEO COORDINATOR TO THE NBA FINALS

One way to get a foot in the door as a scout is to serve as a video coordinator, which is basically a scouting job without the travel.

Video coordinators at both the college and professional levels are responsible for analyzing talent to determine whether players in particular sports are worthy of scholarship offers, draft selections, or free agent signings. But they also work as advance scouts to dissect the tendencies, strengths, and weaknesses of future opponents.

The job of video coordinator can be a stepping-stone to a more extensive scouting career. But it has

(continued on page 46)

San Francisco Giants video coordinator Danny Martin is shown here setting up a camera in the dugout to monitor pitchers and catchers before a spring training game.

(continued from page 45)

also served to further the opportunities for prospective coaches. In fact, two of the most successful head coaches in the NBA began their careers in that league as video coordinators.

One of them is Erik Spoelstra, who gained experience with the Miami Heat as a video coordinator before eventually earning a job as head coach with that organization. Spoelstra led the Heat into the NBA Finals in 2011 before taking them to the top in both 2012 and 2013. Of course, he did get a bit of help from a player named LeBron James.

Another example of a coach that learned the tools of his trade as a video coordinator is Mike Brown, who served in that role with the Denver Nuggets and later became head coach of the Cleveland Cavaliers. Brown guided that team into the 2007 NBA Finals and twice coached the Cavaliers to the best regular season record in the league. Brown, however, cannot take all the credit—he, too, received quite a bit of help from the incredible James.

research the characteristics that could make or break the future of an athlete.

GETTING INSIDE THEIR HEADS

It also takes a bit of an amateur psychologist to thrive as a scout. The understanding of an athlete's emotional state and motivation can prove as important to a successful evaluation as awareness of his physical talents or limitations. An athlete with confidence, passion, drive, and emotional stability can often overcome a lack of top-level physical ability to achieve greatness in college and professional sports. On the other hand, one lacking in those traits might fail despite boasting tremendous athleticism. College students considering a career in scouting would be wise to take courses in psychology and practice using knowledge gained in the classroom to assess the potential of top athletes in their schools. They can even prepare for a future in scouting by projecting the potential of a nonathletic friend or family in college or professional sports based on what they know about them psychologically. Removing the athletic equation establishes a mind-set for evaluating the whole person, not simply the physical talent on the court or field of play.

Both high school and college students are in wonderful positions to do just that. They can take advantage of their proximity to sporting events on campus and passion for sports in which scouts are utilized by attending games with the purpose of analyzing the potential of athletes beyond physical talent. Students considering a scouting career should watch with a different mind-set. Ask yourself the following questions about the top athletes as they go about their business:

- How do they react under pressure with the outcome of games on the line? Do they rise to the occasion or collapse under the weight of that pressure?

- How successfully do they interact with and inspire teammates? Do their body language, verbal interaction, and encouragement inspire their teammates to play better?

- How do they respond to adversity? Do they raise or lower their level of performance when the tide has turned against them and their team? Do they show frustration over

Los Angeles Angels of Anaheim 2013 top draft pick Hunter Green *(right)* is introduced to catcher Chris Iannetta *(back to the camera)* by assistant general manager, scouting, and player development Scott Servais *(middle)*.

questionable calls by umpires of referees and lash out against them or do they take them in stride?

- What kind of relationship have they established with their head coach or manager and his assistants? Are they respectful of their authority? Do they look like they are concentrating and soaking up instructions during timeouts or can you detect their eyes and minds wandering?

There is no better way to experience the job of a scout than by playing the role of one at a live sporting event. But prospective scouts should keep in mind the differences in maturity between high school and college athletes. Nearly all high school athletes are given time not only to hone their physical talents in college or in the minor leagues in baseball and hockey but also to mature as people. College athletes in the NBA and NFL must be ready physically, mentally, and emotionally to play at the professional level. Scouts understand that—and so should those eyeing a scouting career.

Thinking like a scout is the first step to becoming a scout. College students should plug in to every outlet available to them to prepare for a career. That means maximizing academic potential and setting sights on a degree, possibly in sports management. It means becoming immersed in the sport for which you feel the most passion and in which you would like to spend your life as a scout. It means learning about player evaluation through college coaches used to scout high school players and future foes. It means practicing the art of scouting at college sporting events. It means seeking out professional scouts at college football, baseball, basketball, or hockey games and being outgoing and confident enough to ask them about the tools of their trade. Then, before you have even received your diploma on cap-and-gown day, you can begin preparing for an internship or full-time employment as a scout.

Chapter 4
A ROAD WELL TRAVELED

Those considering a career in scouting should ask themselves the following question: how much do I need my sleep? If the answer is "eight hours a night," then think about another line of work. Then they should ask themselves another question: how much do I like to travel? If the answer is "not much," then scouting is definitely not for them. But those who enjoy living out of a suitcase and do not mind grabbing some shut-eye a few hours at a time could be suited perfectly for the lifestyle scouts must embrace, particularly during times of the year in which their sport is active.

Pat Zipfel, who followed a short career as a college basketball coach with a long one as an advance scout for several NBA teams, knows all about that. He chronicled a typical road trip during his time with the Houston Rockets in an article published on the team Web site in January 2009. He led into his itinerary with the following warning:

The life of a sports scout can be a lonely one away from family and friends. Many of them travel all over the country, so the airport is a familiar place.

"Make no mistake—life as an advance scout in the NBA is a grind."

Zipfel awoke at 4:15 AM and left his home in Philadelphia a half-hour later. He drove to the airport, from which his plane took off at 7:30. He managed to get two hours of sleep. It would be his last rest until he could nod off for less than two hours at 2:30 the next morning. The following are some of his recollections between those two short naps.

December 1st, 2008

9:55 AM – Arrive in Denver – Leave Plane 1 and Go Find Gate for second flight

10:48 AM – Boarding begins for Flight 6185 to Oakland, CA

1:10 PM – Arrive in Oakland California

1:25 PM – Head to Ground transportation and Rental Car location

2:00 PM – Drive to Marriott Hotel, Downtown Oakland…

2:40 PM – Head to downtown Oakland Starbucks with laptop – work on statistical preparation for the Warriors

5:30 PM – Drive to Oracle Arena – Home of the Golden State Warriors

6:25 PM – Watch Warmups of players – Paying particular attention to the various NEW Warriors

7:10 PM – Head back to Media Room for dinner

7:30 PM – Game Begins – Golden State Warriors vs Miami Heat

10:00 PM – Game goes into Overtime – and the Heat pull out a victory

10:20 PM – Leave Oracle Arena … fight traffic…

11:10 PM – Plug in laptop and enter plays the Warriors used that night

December 2nd, 2008

1:00 AM – Do Rolling call sheet with Time/Call for our video department and coaches

2:15 AM – Finish Golden State Scouting Report and send to coaches

Zipfel allowed himself two hours of sleep that night before starting the process all over again on a scouting mission in Dallas to watch the Los Angeles Clippers. He got less than three hours of sleep on the plane and his head did not touch a pillow again until the wee hours of the next morning. At 1:30 AM he had begun scouting upcoming opponent Atlanta on video. Zipfel added that he eats nearly all his meals in airports and arena media rooms. He scouted about 150 games during the 2007–2008 season and estimated that he ate dinner in media rooms at least 135 times.

It is difficult for Zipfel to maintain a healthy lifestyle. Good eating habits and time to exercise do not come easy. But his schedule is common for advance scouts in other sports during the season.

Houston Rockets advance scout Pat Zipfel gave an account of his busy travel schedule with an itinerary of a scouting mission in which he provided his team with information about future opponents.

ALWAYS ON THE GO

Also hectic are the lives of MLB and NHL scouts. Scouts for MLB teams become quite familiar with airports and stadiums throughout the United States, as well as in Canada. They are fortunate only in that their teams play three or four games at a time against opponents. Baseball scouts are dispatched to watch hitters and pitchers their teams will be facing in series to come. Like their NBA counterparts, NHL teams play eighty-two games a season. NHL scouts experience a similarly chaotic schedule during the season.

The lighter game schedule and complexities of pro football make scouting in that sport different. Since teams play just once a week in a sixteen-game schedule, the pro scouting departments of NFL franchises work closely with their coaching staffs throughout the week after they have compiled reports from scouting the previous game of an opponent and poring over tapes of games made available to them. Advance NFL scouts are no less busy than their counterparts in other sports are, but their travel schedules are certainly less hectic during the season.

High school and college scouts are also quite familiar with plane travel and nights away from home, though some do not rack up the air mileage of their advance scout counterparts. Professional sports franchises employ area scouts who are assigned to particular

John Sullivan, a scout with the Green Bay Packers, measures the wingspan of Colorado State University's offensive lineman Paul Madsen before football practice. Pro scouts have a keen eye for talent and must know a prospective athlete's every strength and weakness.

regions of the country and beyond. Some baseball scouts are centered in Latin American countries such as the Dominican Republic, where many of the best prospects in the sport have spent their early lives honing their talents for a shot at the big leagues. NBA scouts are sometimes dispatched to Europe, where a growing number of players in the league have established their credentials. NHL scouts evaluate high school and college players in the United States, Canada, and Europe.

Veteran baseball scout Doug Mapson, who has worked with the San Francisco Giants and Chicago Cubs, goes where the action is. Among his destinations is the Cape Cod Summer League in Massachusetts, which annually produces some of the finest young talent in the nation. Mapson understands that he must keep his ears open. He can learn about prospects anywhere, including the hundreds of hours he spends a year flying from one place to the next. Mapson explained that in an interview with *USA Today.* "I get told about players on flights all the time," he remarked. "I listen to all suggestions, try to write down the info and pass it on to the appropriate area scout. I learned long ago that you never know where a solid tip will come from."

Mapson added that he stays in hotels between 150 and 200 nights each year. But he embraces the travel and mystery of what is to come on a daily basis. He never knows when he is about to stumble upon the next baseball superstar.

"Everyone asks me when I'm going to give up all that travel," he said. "As long as I keep getting up in the morning and finding that next great prospect, I want to keep doing it. I love my job."

The thrill of victory is indeed not limited to athletes. Scouts experience it every time their finds blossom into greatness at the top levels of their sports. Mapson knows all about that. In 1984, he helped the Chicago Cubs scout pitcher Greg Maddux, who won an astounding 355 games and four Cy Young Awards, and eventually led the Atlanta Braves to the 1995 World Series championship. It took a keen eye for Mapson to project Maddux to star in the big leagues. After all,

QUITE A SCOUTING REPORT

Baseball fans have seen the replay on television dozens of times. It was Game 1 of the 1988 World Series. The Oakland Athletics were heavy favorites to defeat the Los Angeles Dodgers.

Sensational Oakland closer Dennis Eckersley entered the game in the ninth inning with his team ahead 4–3. He retired the first two batters but walked the third. With one man on base and his team on the verge of defeat, pinch-hitter Kirk Gibson emerged from the dugout and limped to the plate. The battered, aging outfielder was not even supposed to play in the game. He was hobbled by injuries to his hamstring, ankle, and knee. He could barely walk.

The importance of scouting was evident in Game 1 of the 1988 World Series, when Dodgers slugger Kirk Gibson used scouting information about Athletics pitcher Dennis Eckersley to blast a game-winning home run.

The noise level at Dodgers Stadium was deafening at the count reached 3-2. Gibson had looked overmatched flailing away at Eckersley's fastballs. But Gibson remembered the report that Dodgers advance scout Mel Didier had left the team. It stated that the side-arming Eckersley liked to throw a "backdoor" slider to left-handed batters on 3-2 counts. In other words, he tried to sneak that pitch over the outside corner.

(continued on page 60)

(continued from page 59)

Sure enough, Didier was right. Eckersley threw that exact pitch. Gibson reached out and slammed the ball into the right-field seats for the game-winning home run. He pumped his arm twice in celebration as he rounded the bases. It was not only one of the most dramatic moments in baseball history, but it showed the importance of a keen and experienced scout.

The Dodgers took the momentum and ran with it to a four-game sweep of the Athletics in one of the greatest upsets in World Series history. It was Didier's scouting report on Eckersley that proved to be the catalyst.

the right-hander did not throw a blazing fastball. He thrived on guile, changing speeds on his pitches, and pinpoint control. Mapson later scouted fellow right-handed pitcher Tim Lincecum, who helped the San Francisco Giants win two world titles. Such triumphs for a scout make all the travel worthwhile.

CHECK YOUR EGO AT THE DOOR

Scouting is indeed not a nine-to-five job. It is not a forty-hours-a-week job. It is also not a self-serving job. Those who yearn to be thrust into the spotlight should shy away from scouting. Scouts and coaches who scout must understand they are working as a team for the betterment of their high school or college athletics department or professional franchise. Information about talented young players must be shared with colleagues. The old expression "there is no 'I' in 'team'" is particularly appropriate in the scouting business. Baseball scout Michael Juhl, who has worked with the St. Louis Cardinals, Baltimore Orioles, Boston Red Sox, Chicago White Sox, and Texas Rangers, is keenly aware of that. He is also aware that one of the prerequisites for success as a scout is organization and an ability to change schedules without losing your cool.

"Juggling schedules of all the high school and colleges in an area is a daunting task," Juhl explained in an interview with the author. "You also have to be able to adapt on the fly. Weather, injuries and re-directs from the office tend to make that 'perfect' schedule imperfect."

Though there is satisfaction in scouting and recommending a player who blossoms at the college or professional level, there is equal disappointment when a player fails to live up to expectations. Scouts must remain confident in their ability despite occasional setbacks and be selfless enough to deflect credit. Owners, general managers, coaches, and managers are commended by the media and fans for astute drafting and free agent signings. Scouts, who initiate the interest in players based on experience and analysis, are usually overlooked when praise is passed around.

The same is true for advance scouts, who go unappreciated by everyone but the coaches and players who benefit from the reports about how best to defend and attack opponents. Even though teams by which they are employed understand their value, advance scouts go unseen and unheard by the players that profit from their work. To the players, advance scouts are nothing but the authors of words on a piece of paper. Zipfel described his feeling of anonymity in an article on the Houston Rockets Web site.

"Every night another city and another game," he wrote. "Traveling alone. Imagine this—our players and coaches have not seen me since the last day of training camp [about three months earlier]! In fact, most of our players don't even know who I am but somehow reports end up on their locker room chairs on game days. If they only knew the process it took to get that information. Flights, hotels, cab rides and some funny stories along the way.

The glamorous life of being an Advance NBA Scout? Waking up and not knowing what city you are in…"

Zipfel touched upon perhaps the most compelling aspect of his job and that of every professional, college, and high school scout. The prospect of watching and

NBA commissioner David Stern poses with the 2013 draft class. The NBA draft lasts just two rounds and is limited to college and international players.

analyzing the finest athletes in the world or evaluating young athletes toiling to reach that status is indeed the most fascinating and fun part of scouting. A passion and appreciation for the sport one is scouting is a requirement for those who yearn to maximize the enjoyment of working in the profession. Those who truly love their sport will always marvel at the talents of the players they scout.

Yet scouts must always temper their admiration for the athletic talents that they are witnessing with the understanding that they are in attendance to do a job. That job is complex and sport specific. Scouts in all sports must analyze far beyond general traits of athleticism, such as speed, quickness, and power into the realm of emotional stability and mental aptitude.

Only when the lifestyle and job description of a scout are understood should anyone begin a quest in earnest to seek out a job or internship in the profession. And that task must be achieved with the same passion and diligence that the best scouts display in their work every day.

Chapter 5

PATH TO A SCOUTING CAREER

Some prospective scouts need not make a pitch to professional sports franchises. They are the coaches and players who have already been employed by their organizations and who have displayed the intelligence and insight to be hired as scouts without a great deal of convincing. All other candidates, particularly recent college graduates, must make themselves known to employers in the sports world and prove impressive enough to land an internship or job.

Perhaps the most realistic path to a scouting career is to spend time as a coach in the sport with which you are most familiar and have played, preferably at the college level. Major college football staffs, in particular, are peppered with graduate assistants seeking to work their way up the coaching ranks. Though baseball, basketball, hockey, and soccer teams have smaller coaching staffs, they quite often employ graduate assistants, too.

Prospective scouts should make their intentions known while in college to use experience as a coach as a stepping-stone to a career in scouting. A chat with the athletics director or head coach in any of those sports will direct you to the proper channels one must pass through at that particular school to land a job as a graduate coaching assistant.

That could lead to a full-time job as a coach, which is perhaps the surest method of securing a scouting career. It also creates two viable options. Those who enjoy college coaching and are deemed effective in their work can secure a lifetime of scouting as well. College coaches double as scouts and recruiters for their programs. They not only toil to identify the premier high school talent in the country but can also serve as advance scouts assessing the strengths, weaknesses, and tendencies of future opponents.

College students can take many paths to a career in scouting, but some involvement in sports is a must. Shown here are equipment managers at work at Purdue University.

Those who still yearn to work at the highest levels of sports as a college recruiter or advance scout in such leagues as the NFL, NBA, NHL, or MLB can use their experience as a college coach as a springboard to a scouting career in one of those leagues.

Having played a sport is sometimes a prerequisite for those seeking to be hired as a college coach who scouts or as a professional sports scout. Landing an undergraduate degree or even a master's in sports management or sports administration, learning directly from scouts and honing one's scouting skills through practice at high school or college sporting events, are not always enough to secure an internship or job in the field. Some employers believe that players and coaches understand best the intricacies of every position on the court or field and are therefore the most qualified scouts.

But Ourlads Scouting Service general manager Dan Shonka gives encouragement to those simply not talented enough as an athlete to compete in the sport of their choice at the high school or college level, yet still yearn for a career in scouting. "Playing experience is nice, as it gives you an 'on field' understanding of the game ... but it is not a necessity," Shonka noted in an interview with the author.

Coaching, however, is also not a viable path for everyone, particularly college graduates who have not played a sport at that level. Even those who have lent their services as a volunteer scout or have served in some other off-the-field capacity for a college sports

Mike Stoeber, who works in the football technology department of the Jacksonville Jaguars, is seen here addressing potential scouts for Sports Management Worldwide.

team or athletics department are far less likely to land a coaching job than are those with playing experience.

Prospective scouts who cannot use coaching as a catalyst should not be discouraged. The best method of working your way into the business is through what is in baseball terms called "bird dogging." That process begins by creating a résumé that highlights your experience as a player, coach, or volunteer scout in the sport in which you are most interested and qualified. If you are considering a career in basketball, for instance, there is no point in emphasizing your experience in football.

TAKE A SCOUT TO DINNER

The next step is to identify and befriend a scout that works often in your region of the country. Professional franchises at the highest levels often employ many scouts in areas richest with talent in that sport. For instance, MLB teams will flood regions such as southern California and Florida with scouts but perhaps employ just one scout to cover the New England states. Finding a scout in areas with fewer prospects is more difficult, but it must be stressed that every top-level professional sports organization employs scouts in all areas. Prospective scouts should seek out mentors at events they know feature the finest athletes. They need not establish contact face-to-face. Once a scout is identified, a call or e-mail expressing a desire to become part of the profession could lead to a meeting at a sporting event to discuss and learn more about the business. Emphasize your desire to become a scout. Scouts are generally

flattered that others think enough of their work to want to follow in their footsteps.

It is important to show confidence upon meeting a scout. Your experience in that sport is valuable. Give your

Potential baseball scouts learning the tools of the trade as part of the Major League Baseball Scouting Development Program soak in action in the Dominican Republic.

scout your résumé but also express verbally how you can benefit an organization. Show the scout any player analysis you have created in high school or college, as well as any positive feedback you have received from coaches. You must convince scouts of your usefulness. Ask if you can sit with the scout and evaluate players, then share your thoughts. You will find it not only a fine learning experience but also a chance to match your scouting skills with those of a professional. Create a written report and send it to the scout for a critique.

You can cement a positive relationship with scouts by identifying area prospects in their sports and volunteering to analyze their talents and project their college or professional potential. That is where the "bird dogging" and your real experience as a scout begins. If you are successful in finding a viable prospect, the scout could recommend you for associate status and at least a stipend from his organization.

He might also recommend you for placement in a scouting school. Perhaps the most notable is the MLB Scout Development Program, run by the MLB Scouting Bureau. The school convenes for a two-week course every fall in Phoenix, Arizona. Students must be sponsored by a major league team, which certainly limits opportunities and increases the need to convince a scout that you are worthy of inclusion. But once you have been selected

Veteran basketball scouts *(from left to right)* Scotty Stirling, Frank Burlison, and Ed Gregory teach Sports Management Worldwide students about how to forge a career in the business.

THE LIFE OF A GRADUATE ASSISTANT

There are several paths on the road to a job as a football scout, but one of the most effective ways to reach your goal is to become a college coach. One of the surest ways to launch that career is to become a graduate assistant.

Graduate assistants are full-time students working on their master's degree, sometimes in sports management. They are often former players seeking a coaching career, which would allow them to scout at the high school level or serve as an advance scout. But some are also looking for a way to land a job as a scout with an NFL team. There is arguably no better way to gain insight into college player evaluation than to coach at that level.

Many college football programs utilize one graduate assistant who specializes on offense and another on defense. Others can work as a video coordinator, but National College Athletic Association rules dictate a maximum of two graduate assistants in any program.

Most graduate assistants played the sport in college, but not on a high level. It is also common for nonplayers to work their way into coaching as a graduate assistant after having worked with the team in some capacity as an undergraduate. Some full-time coaches with small college teams accept a graduate assistant position with a major program to better position themselves for a coaching or scouting career.

Graduate assistants play major roles on their teams. They often coach players or units (such as linebackers or running backs) and can prepare for a career in scouting by evaluating talent on video, though they are not allowed to travel on scouting missions. They can also be greatly responsible for preparing a game plan against an opponent they have assessed on video. They often spend the Sundays and Mondays after games helping make preparations for the next opponent.

to participate, you are well on your way to a career as a baseball scout.

Among those fortunate to have earned a spot was Brian Boles, who toiled as a high school baseball coach in Maryland. He worked with a scout who recommended him to the Detroit Tigers. Boles had proven his talents by successfully scouting players for the Tigers in his state, which motivated the team to sponsor him for inclusion in the Scout Development Program. Boles, who had helped build a baseball facility in the inner city of Washington, D.C., wrote an article about his experience in 2011 for the Center for Neighborhood Enterprise. He detailed a typical day in Phoenix as a combination of morning meetings, attendance at games for scouting practice, report writing, and personal time with an instructor to review the scouting reports. Boles wrote the following about the value of the program:

> *The Major League Scouting Bureau's Scouting Development Program was everything I expected it to be and more. My goal was to get better every day and learn as much as possible. . . . We covered various topics such as scout code of conduct, what to look for in a player, formula for judgment and organizing your territory, to name a few. . . . In the words of MLSB director Frank Marcos, "you only get one shot with integrity." This is a good character trait for a baseball scout, but an even better one for being a great person.*

MLB has taken the lead in scout development with its live school. The NFL, NBA, and NHL do not offer such hands-on courses, but online organizations do provide an education that can bolster a résumé and help land a job with a professional franchise. Perhaps the most prominent is Sports Management Worldwide, which features an eight-week online class for prospective basketball, football, and hockey scouts. The course, however, is not specifically designed to groom only scouts. It also emphasizes teaching students about the position of general manager. But among the instructors in the course are those with extensive scouting experience in their particular sports. The three sport-specific options allow prospective scouts to learn about the profession in which they are most interested and experienced.

Once you have earned your college degree and further credentials, which could include playing and coaching a sport, volunteering to scout high school and college games, landing an internship, working with area scouts, or taking scouting classes, you are ready to seek full-time employment. Former University of Texas football coach Darrell Royal expressed in *The Comprehensive Guide to Careers in Sports*, written by Glenn Wong, what could be the creed for prospective scouts working to land their first good job. "Luck is what happens when preparation meets opportunity," he said.

Professional sports organizations are inundated with résumés for a wide variety of positions, including scouting. They are flooded with inquiries about a limited number of openings. The most qualified are chosen for interviews. Furthermore, unless there are multiple openings, just one is selected for each.

CONFIDENCE IS THE KEY

Prospective scouts should be confident that the work they have put in will bear fruit. But they cannot skimp on the final process of securing a job, which can be painstaking, even in this computer-driven era.

The following question should be asked before the first step is taken: are you willing to move anywhere in

Developing positive relationships is critical to success in scouting. Only through friendly contact can scouts earn the trust of those who provide valuable information about prospective talent.

the United States or Canada to secure work as a scout? In a field with painfully few openings that are filled only by the most qualified and experienced candidates, many of whom are former players and coaches, limiting oneself to one's hometown or one particular area of the United States can prove self-defeating. It is far easier to target one familiar and comfortable region of the country in other areas of the sports industry. You must remember that scouts are going to travel extensively anyway. Scouts might live in the location of the franchise, but they are quite unlikely to spend much time there. The travel associated with scouting is an adventure. Only those who embrace it can thrive.

Once you have accepted the probability of relocation, the task of landing a job begins. Before the arrival of personal computers, e-mail, and the Internet, prospective scouts were forced to learn about job openings through interaction with established scouts and a series of phone calls to professional organizations. That communication you have hopefully created with one or more scouts certainly remains an excellent pipeline to openings within his organization and beyond. After all, scouts have likely developed relationships with rival scouts who can tip them off about job openings within their franchises.

The search for a job can also be achieved at home through individual team Web sites. But even if there are no listed openings for a scout, you should flood the market with your résumé and cover letter sent to the scouting departments of every franchise in your targeted sport. Each of those correspondences should be followed up with a phone call. It is also wise to ask the scout you have befriended to contact his department to put in a good word for you. Personal recommendations from a scout trusted by his organization can prove more valuable than any résumé.

A strong résumé, however, is important. Personal experiences in playing, coaching, and scouting in a particular sport should be emphasized on a résumé. Those who show the perseverance of attaining a college degree impress employers, but the knowledge of a sport gained through competing and evaluating talent separates the unqualified candidate from the superior one. Most scouting directors will hire only those with familiarity of player assessment. Such expertise must be highlighted on a résumé.

Another critical step is to compile a list of references, which should if possible include only those who have benefitted from your scouting experience. High school, college, and professional scouts with whom you have worked, particularly in the sport you are targeting, are essential references. High school and college athletics directors and coaches who can testify to your playing, coaching, and scouting experience and talents should also be listed. Positive quotes from any of them about your work ethic and ability can prove beneficial.

They do not usually secure a job, however. The final step is an engaging and convincing interview with a potential employer. At that point, you are on the verge of landing a scouting position for which you have likely been yearning for years. You must put your best foot forward by being as prepared as possible. A thorough knowledge of the sport, the scouting process, and the franchise for which you would be working are all essential elements to a successful interview.

Every team, after all, is unique. Those seeking employment with those teams should study their histories and, in particular, their current personnel on the field or court. Certain franchises have earned reputations for standout characteristics. The Los Angeles Dodgers, for instance, have been known for their great pitching for generations. The NFL Chicago Bears are a storied franchise because of their defense. It is wise for anyone being interviewed by a team for a scouting job to understand the team's history and speak intelligently about it. It is also wise to know its current strengths and weaknesses and assure the employer that you have the scouting savvy to maintain those strengths and eliminate the weaknesses.

Confidence is critical. Moreover, knowledge breeds confidence. Nervousness is natural during interviews, but knowledge is the best antidote. The interviewer will be impressed by the fact that you boast a thorough knowledge of his organization. But he will also want to ensure that, concerning any sport in question, you are well versed in what a scout looks for in players. Those considering a scouting career at the professional sports level must also understand the structure of the league for which they are most interested in working.

Chapter 6

EYE ON THE PRESENT AND THE FUTURE

Job opportunities in scouting are certainly more restrictive than in other lines of work in sports. There are no scouts in high school sports. There are no scouts in college sports. Though college coaches serve as high school and advance scouts, their athletics programs employ no full-time scouts. There are no scouts in the lower levels of team sports such as minor league baseball, hockey, or basketball. There are no scouts in such individual professional sports such as tennis, golf, or bowling. There are no scouts in amateur sports such as gymnastics or figure skating.

There is a ray of sunshine, however, peeking through what might be considered a dark cloud. Though there are fewer overall jobs in scouting, the fact that they are centralized allows prospects to focus on one sport and one league. Every league in the major North American sports—baseball, football, basketball, and hockey—boasts at least thirty franchises. In addition, independent scouting services in those sports provide more opportunities, though it should be understood that they generally employ experienced scouts.

It should be noted, however, that a drastic increase in the number of scouting jobs is not expected in the future. Expansion in the 1970s and 1980s in all major sports leagues resulted in dozens of new teams and the necessity to hire hundreds of new scouts. But the expansion era has ended. Though the NFL, the NBA, the NHL, and MLB could add franchises down the road, it is unlikely there will be a dramatic boost.

SOME PROFESSIONAL LEAGUE FACTORS

Examining each major professional league and future prospects for those seeking work in scouting will present you with some of the following facts about each.

BASEBALL

- MLB is divided into a National League and American League, each of which features fifteen teams that employ dozens of scouts. Each league is separated into three divisions with five teams each.

- Because both high school and college players are eligible to be selected in the

Washington Nationals scouts Pablos Arias *(center left)* and Carlos Ulloa *(center right)* instruct players during a weekly tryout in the Dominican Republic. Few athletes make it to the top, but experience in the sport can prove vital to landing a job as a scout for a team.

annual amateur draft, MLB scouts evaluate players competing in both levels.

- A director of scouting and several assistants who help direct the scouts in the field lead the scouting department of each team.

- Scouts for each team are assigned a territory in which to assess high school or college talent. All teams place their largest number of scouts in areas of the country that boast the top prospects. Since baseball is a year-round sport in warm-weather areas such as Florida, Arizona,

Texas, and Southern California, many scouts are assigned in those areas. But every organization has the country covered.

- The tremendous foreign baseball talent and the growing popularity of the sport outside the United States have forced organizations to employ scouts in other countries. It is an advantage for prospective scouts to learn to speak Spanish, Japanese, or Korean. The influx of players into the major leagues in recent decades has been centered in Latin America and, to a lesser degree, Japan and Korea. MLB is also trying to cultivate the sport in Europe. Players who have competed outside the realm of American colleges and high schools are not eligible for the draft, but they can be signed by major league teams as free agents.

FOOTBALL

- The National Football League (NFL) is divided into the American Football Conference (AFC) and National Football Conference (NFC). Each conference boasts sixteen franchises separated into four divisions of four teams.

- The NFL does not scout high school players. The league mandates that only players who have competed at the college level for three years are eligible for the draft, which is held annually in late April.

- Like their baseball brethren, football scouts are dispatched to areas of the country rich with talent. But though "football factories" in such states as Florida, California, and Texas churn out huge numbers of NFL players every decade, the talent in this sport is more spread out than it is in baseball. Schools in states that do not produce a large number of MLB players, such as Ohio State, Syracuse, Nebraska, and Oklahoma, have traditionally placed many players into the NFL.

- The Canadian Football League (CFL) provides another option for potential scouts, but there are certainly fewer opportunities. The league boasts just eight teams—four in the East Division and four in the West Division. The rules of the sport are also a bit different. Scouts seeking employment with a CFL team must be well aware of those differences.

BASKETBALL

- The NBA is separated into the Eastern Conference and Western Conference, both of which feature three divisions of five teams each.

Scouts often evaluate minor league players for possible promotion into the NBA. Such scouts are shown here at a Developmental League game between Dakota and Rio Grande.

- From 1995 to 2005, high school graduates were eligible for the annual NBA draft in June. But the collective bargaining agreement between the players and league have since mandated that amateurs must compete in at least one year at the college level or have played professional basketball outside the country to be eligible for the draft.

- Basketball is the most international of the major American sports and the talent inside the country is arguably the most spread out,

though much of it is centered in the major cities. NBA teams employ many of their scouts in such metropolitan areas as New York, Chicago, Detroit, Philadelphia, Los Angeles, Houston, and Miami. But they cover all regions of the United States for less-publicized players and keep a sharp eye for talent outside the country, particularly in Eastern Europe, South America and even China. Prospective scouts who speak the languages of countries in those areas of the world could have an advantage in the NBA, which has sought to expand its global base.

HOCKEY

- The NHL is divided into the Eastern Conference and Western Conference. Both house three divisions of five teams each.

- Hockey is the national pastime of the United States' northern neighbor, where six of the NHL franchises reside. More future NHL talent performs in Canada than in any other country in the world.

• The popularity of hockey extends beyond North America, but not around the globe. Scouts flood the colleges and youth leagues throughout the United States and Canada, but they also keep a keen eye out for the exceptional amateur hockey talent in the Scandinavian countries, in Eastern Europe, and throughout Russia. European players are prominent among the team selections of the annual NHL draft, which is held in

Many scouts attend the NHL Prospects Tournament, such as this one played in Traverse City, Michigan. Watching the top prospects in one event is an attraction scouts would not miss.

late June. The first ten picks of the 2013 draft, for instance, included two players from Finland, one from Sweden, one from Russia, and just one from the United States. The other five were Canadian.

So what do scouts look for in a player? That depends on the sport and the position. The physical, mental, and emotional necessities of athletes vary. The first baseman on a baseball team does not require the quickness of a second baseman but is generally expected to boast more power. A power forward on a basketball team does not need to dribble or pass the ball as well as the point guard. A free safety on a football team does not require the brute strength of a defensive lineman. The complexities of every position in every sport explain why scouts specialize in one sport.

That understanding of the game means an understanding of every facet of every position in the game. It also means understanding the difference between what is sought in a high school athlete as opposed to a college athlete.

It is far more difficult, for instance, for a baseball scout to project the production of a high school pitcher than a college pitcher. The high school pitcher has likely not fully developed all his breaking pitchers, such as a curveball or a slider, whereas a scout must see good movement on such pitches from a college pitcher to recommend drafting him.

SHOOTING FOR THE TOP

Though many scouts enjoy the job and the lifestyle so thoroughly that they are content to remain in their jobs throughout their careers, others yearn to maximize their potential within their organizations. Some have succeeded in working their way up into the general manager (GM) position.

The job of GM pays far more than that of any in the scouting department, such as director of player personnel or director of scouting. It also allows scouts to settle down and eliminate nearly all the travel that could often take a toll on their personal and family lives.

Among those who have completed the journey from scout to GM in baseball were Jack Zduriencik (Seattle Mariners) and Mike Rizzo (Washington Nationals).

Draft picks such as Seattle Mariners 2012 No. 1 selection Mike Zunino *(center)* receive great attention. He was introduced here by scouting director Tom McNamara *(left)* and general manager Jack Zduriencik.

Zduriencik toiled as a minor league second baseman in the Chicago White Sox minor league system and coached at the college level before working as an area scout and scouting director. He landed his GM job in 2009. Rizzo got his feet wet as a minor league player in the California Angels system before embarking on a twenty-five-year career as a scout and scouting director. He became a GM in 2010.

It can be assumed that scouts in all sports rooted for the two to gain success as general managers because they opened up doors for all scouts. If they proved they could make the transition from scout to GM, other organizations in baseball and throughout the major sports world would be open to make similar hires.

"Maybe there will be a realization that there is a value into what the eyes see," said Zduriencik in a 2010 Fox Sports article written by Tracy Ringolsby titled "Future GMs Might Come from Scouting Ranks." Zduriencik showed his worth as scouting director when his team used first-round picks on future superstars Prince Fielder and Ryan Braun.

A scout must also project added weight and strength from a high school hitter, who will likely add power as he plays minor league baseball. College hitters not strong enough to hit home runs consistently are unlikely to become power hitters at the highest professional level, though they can develop some power along the way.

The same is true in all sports. High school athletes—aside from incredible exceptions such as NBA superstar LeBron James—are simply not developed enough physically, mentally, or emotionally to perform against the best in the world. That makes the work of a high school scout particularly difficult. It also makes the job quite stressful for baseball scouts, who spend more time evaluating high school talent than their counterparts in any other American sport. Because high school football and basketball players are ineligible for the draft, only baseball and hockey scouts work at the prep level.

THE PRESSURE OF GETTING IT RIGHT

The relative lack of money offered to the top players in decades past resulted in less pressure on scouts to project high school players with pinpoint accuracy. But in this era of multimillion-dollar contracts for the premier high school talent, the scouts must be right or their jobs could be in jeopardy. Even though MLB has gone to a slotting system that helps determine the bonuses given to draft picks, the contracts remain huge for the best prep players. For instance, the bonus the Minnesota Twins gave high school pitcher Kohl Stewart, whom they selected with the fourth pick in the 2013 draft, was more than $4.5 million.

That means it is important not only to assess correctly the physical skills of a prospect but their mental and

Signing a first major league contract is a proud moment for a player such as Minnesota Twins 2013 top draft pick Kohl Stewart. Also signing his name to the contract is general manager Terry Ryan.

emotional makeup as well. The high-tech world of baseball scouting has added tools such as radar guns to determine the speed of a pitch and computers to help scouts compare the physical talents of one player against the next. But one aspect of the scout's job will never change. That is, scouts must be judges of character. Character helps determine how a prospect reacts under pressure and responds to failure. And there is no computer in the world that can help scouts make that evaluation. Just ask longtime scout J. P. Ricciardi, who went on to serve as general manager of the Toronto Blue Jays and spoke on the subject to ESPN.com sportswriter Sean McAdam. "The kid with a lot of talent is going to have success," Ricciardi conceded. "But it's the intangibles that can make the difference. You almost have to be a little bit of a detective these days. You have to dig and find out."

What do you have to find out? Tom Mooney, who has worked as a scout for the Seattle Mariners, Houston Astros, and Milwaukee Brewers, explained that to McAdam. "Scouts are spending more time in the home with Mom and Dad," Mooney said. "A lot of teams are giving different tests, trying to figure out what kind of kid they're dealing with. More and more, mental makeup is very important.

…When you are watching a 17 year old kid who's dominating at the high school level, as a scout you have to take him off that high school field and think about him in the [minor leagues] competing against the best kids from Florida, California, and Texas. What happens when he has his first long slump? Does he give up? Does he work harder?"

In that respect, scouts are like athletes. They, too, are inevitably going to taste failure. All scouts have projected greatness on athletes that have failed and rejected those who have thrived at the professional level. The ability to remain confident and competent under adversity can make the difference between the most successful and least successful scouts in any sport.

Indeed, scouts must pass many mental and emotional tests. It is among the most stressful and challenging jobs

Houston Rockets scout Rudy Tomjanovich follows the action intently as he evaluates players from Ohio State and Penn State during a Big Ten Men's Basketball Tournament.

in the sports world. But it is also among the most reward-ing. There is no greater feeling than rightly projecting greatness for a prospect that other scouts had rejected and knowing that you are part of a team working together to win championships.

"It is not just one scout or one coach that makes a pros-pect," said St. Louis Cardinals director of player personnel Matt Slater, when interviewed by the author. "It is the whole organizational process and we each play a part in it."

It is that outlook that has made the Cardinals one of the premier franchises in sports. What's more, it is that attitude that makes the selfless scout one of the greatest assets to an organization. They do not attract the spotlight. They just perform one of the most impor-tant jobs in sports.

EDUCATIONAL OPPORTUNITIES IN SPORTS SCOUTING

MLB SCOUTING BUREAU SCOUTING DEVELOPMENT PROGRAM

This program is unique in that it is the only live school for prospective scouts in the United States. The two-week program, which runs annually in late September and early October in Phoenix, Arizona, covers every aspect of the job, including evaluation of players at all positions and writing reports.

Admission as a student must be accompanied by sponsorship by a major league team. That is best achieved through recommendation from a scout employed by that organization with which a potential student has worked.

SPORTS MANAGEMENT WORLDWIDE GENERAL MANAGER AND SCOUTING COURSES

Sports Management Worldwide offers eight-week online classes for prospective general managers and scouts in baseball, football, basketball, and hockey. Though none of the courses are scout-specific, portions of the curriculum are taught by experienced scouts in all of those sports.

The intent of the program is to teach students enough about the specifics of player evaluation for them to become a viable aid to a scout, thereby developing a relationship that can lead to employment.

PRO EDGE SPORTS SCOUTING AND OPERATIONS COURSES

Pro Edge features scout-specific online courses for students interested in learning the business in football, soccer, and baseball. The eight-week courses are taught by experienced scouts in those particular sports.

Among the subjects taught to prospective football scouts are duties and responsibilities of a football scout, NFL draft philosophies, creating a scouting report, position by position breakdown of what a scout looks for in a player, and the intricacies of the college bargaining agreement between the NFL players and the league.

COLLEGE AND UNIVERSITY PROGRAMS IN SPORTS MANAGEMENT AND ADMINISTRATION

Arkansas State University
Jonesboro, Arkansas
Bachelor's degree in sports management

Ball State University
Muncie, Indiana
Bachelor's degree in sports administration

Baylor University
Waco, Texas
Master's degree in sports management

Bowling Green State University
Bowling Green, Ohio
Bachelor's and master's degrees in sports management, recreation, and tourism, leisure and event planning

Columbia University
New York, New York
Master's degree in sports management

DePaul University
Chicago, Illinois
Master's degree in sports management

Drexel University
Philadelphia, Pennsylvania
Master's degree in sports management

Eastern Michigan University
Ypsilanti, Michigan
Master's degree in sports management

Florida Atlantic University
Boca Raton, Florida
Master's degree in sports management

Florida State University
Tallahassee, Florida
Bachelor's degree, master's degree, and Ph.D. in sports management

Georgetown University
Washington, D.C.

Master's degree in sports industry management

George Washington University
Washington, D.C.
Master's degree in sports management

Howard University
Washington, D.C.
Bachelor's degree in sports management

Indiana State University
Terre Haute, Indiana
Bachelor's degree and master's degree in sports management

Indiana University
Bloomington, Indiana
Bachelor's degree, master's degree, and Ph.D. in athletics administration and sports management

Kent State University
Kent, Ohio
Bachelor's degree and master's degree in sports administration and sports and recreation management

Liberty University
Lynchburg, Virginia
Bachelor's degree and master's degree in sports management

Louisiana State University
Baton Rouge, Louisiana
Bachelor's degree and master's degree in sports management

Loyola University
Chicago, Illinois
Master's degree in sports management

Marietta College
Marietta, Ohio
Bachelor's degree in sports management

Michigan State University
East Lansing, Michigan
Master's degree in sports administration

Minnesota State University
Mankato, Minnesota
Master's degree in sports management

Mississippi State University
Mississippi State, Mississippi

Master's degree in sports management

Missouri State University
Springfield, Missouri
Master's degree in sports management

New York University
New York, New York
Bachelor's degree in sports management

North Carolina State University
Raleigh, North Carolina
Bachelor's degree in sports management

Northwestern University
Chicago, Illinois
Master's degree in sports administration

Ohio State University
Columbus, Ohio
Master's degree and Ph.D. in sports management

Ohio University
Athens, Ohio
Master's degree in athletics administration

Oklahoma State University
Stillwater, Oklahoma
Bachelor's degree in sports management and sports administration

Old Dominion University
Norfolk, Virginia
Bachelor's degree and master's degree in sports management

Purdue University
West Lafayette, Indiana
Master's degree in recreation and sports management

Rice University
Houston, Texas
Bachelor's degree in sports management

Rutgers University
New Brunswick, New Jersey
Bachelor's degree in sports management

St. Bonaventure University
St. Bonaventure, New York
Bachelor's degree in sports studies/sports management

St. John's University
Queens, New York
Bachelor's degree and master's
  degree in sports management

Sam Houston State University
Huntsville, Texas
Master's degree in kinesiology/
  sports management

San Diego State University
San Diego, California
Master's degree in sports busi-
  ness management

Seton Hall University
South Orange, New Jersey
Bachelor's degree and master's
  degree in sports management

Southern Methodist University
Dallas, Texas
Bachelor's degree and
  master's degree in sports
  management

Temple University
Philadelphia, Pennsylvania
Master's degree in sports and
  recreation management

Texas A&M University
College Station, Texas
Bachelor's degree, master's

degree, and Ph.D. in sports
management

University of Arkansas
Fayetteville, Arkansas
Bachelor's degree and master's
  degree in recreation and
  sports management

University of Connecticut
Storrs, Connecticut
Bachelor's degree, master's
  degree, and Ph.D. in sports
  management

University of Florida
Gainesville, Florida
Bachelor's degree, master's
  degree, and Ph.D. in sports
  management

University of Massachusetts
Amherst, Massachusetts
Bachelor's degree, master's
  degree, and Ph.D. in sports
  management

University of Michigan
Ann Arbor, Michigan
Bachelor's degree in sports
  management

University of North Carolina
Chapel Hill, North Carolina
Bachelor's degree in exercise

and sports science/sports administration

University of Ottawa
Ottawa, Ontario, Canada
Bachelor's degree, master's degree, and Ph.D. in sports management

University of San Francisco
San Francisco, California
Master's degree in sports management

University of Tampa
Tampa, Florida
Bachelor's degree in sports management

University of Texas
Austin, Texas
Bachelor's degree, master's degree, and Ph.D. in sports management

University of Utah
Salt Lake City, Utah
Bachelor's degree in community recreation and sports management

Washington State University
Pullman, Washington
Master's degree in sports management

COLLEGES THAT OFFER ONLINE PROGRAMS

American Military University
Charles Town, West Virginia
Master's degree in sports management

American Public University
Charles Town, West Virginia
Master's degree in sports management, graduate certificate in sports management, graduate certificate in athletics administration

Ashford University
Clinton, Iowa
Bachelor's degree in sports and recreation management

California University at Pennsylvania Online
California, Pennsylvania
Bachelor's degree in sports management, master's degree in sports management studies

Drexel University
Philadelphia, Pennsylvania
Master's degree in sports management

Full Sail University
Winter Park, Florida
Master's degree in sports
  management

Grand Canyon University
Phoenix, Arizona
Bachelor's degree in business
  administration and sports
  management

Lasell College
Newtonville, Massachusetts
Master's degree in sports
  management

Liberty University
Lynchburg, Virginia
Master's degree in sports
  management

Northeastern University
Boston, Massachusetts
Master's degree in sports
  leadership

Post University
Waterbury, Connecticut
Bachelor's degree in sports
  management

St. Leo University
St. Leo, Florida
Master's degree in sports
  management

Southern New Hampshire
  University
Manchester, New Hampshire
Bachelor's degree in sports
  management

Tiffin University
Tiffin, Ohio
Bachelor's degree in sports
  and recreation management

A CAREER IN SPORTS SCOUTING AT A GLANCE

ACADEMICS

- High school degree
- Bachelor's degree, sports management preferred

EXPERIENCE

- Participation in targeted sport
- Work with college recruiter or professional scout
- Scouting practice at sporting events
- Providing information about area athletes to recruiters and scouts

CAREER PATHS

- Coaching as a graduate assistant
- Bird dogging for professional scouts

- Working as college coach and recruiter

- Working as high school or college coach with professional team

- Advance scouting for professional organization

- Volunteering

DUTIES AND RESPONSIBILITIES

- Find and identify prospects

- Judge sport-specific physical talent

- Project prospects of athlete at higher levels

- Identify emotional and mental strengths and weaknesses of athletes

- Judge tendencies of future opponents

- Write scouting reports

SPORTS SCOUTS

SIGNIFICANT POINTS

- There are several types of sports scouting. Those whose job title is "scout" work for professional sports organizations. Most of them evaluate high school or college players to determine whether they are worthy of being drafted or signed as free agents.

- Advance scouts at the professional level watch games played by future opponents live or on tape to assess strengths, weaknesses, and tendencies. They then report back to their teams to discuss the best way to attack or defend that opponent.

- College coaches, particularly in major sports such as football and basketball, serve as scouts and recruiters. They evaluate high school players for possible scholarship offers and attend games played by future foes as advance scouts to prepare for an upcoming meeting on the field or court.

- Scouts not only assess the physical talents of a high school or college player in projecting their production at a higher level but also analyze his mental abilities and emotional makeup to determine potential.

- National Football League and National Basketball Association scouts do not evaluate high school players because they are ineligible for their drafts. MLB and National Hockey League organizations extensively scout high school players, who are eligible to be selected in their drafts.

- All major American sports also keep an eye on talent where that sport thrives internationally. Baseball scouts can be placed in Latin America while hockey and basketball scouts can be sent to Europe. Most of the hockey talent in the NHL is developed in Canada.

NATURE OF THE WORK

Scouts in any sport are assigned territories. They become learned about the talent in their particular areas. The more top prospects that emerge from a particular region of the country, the more scouts are assigned to that region.

Advance scouts in all sports not only evaluate future opponents but are also often sent to watch individual players on other teams for possible trades and free agent acquisitions.

According to the Bureau of Labor Statistics (BLS), a scout's responsibilities include reading newspapers and other news sources to find athletes to consider; attending games, viewing videotapes of the athletes' performances, and studying statistics about the athletes to determine talent and potential; talking to the athlete's coach to see if the athlete has what it takes to be successful; reporting to the coach, manager, or owner of the team for which he or she is scouting; and arranging for and offering incentives to prospective players.

TRAINING

Practicing scouting at high school and college sporting events is essential to developing the skills needed to become a scout. High school and college students should scout and produce reports for coaches and scouts to grade and critique.

The BLS also emphasizes the importance for a coach or scout to boast a thorough knowledge of the sport, which is most often attained through participation as a player. It specifies that scouting often requires playing experience at the college or even professional level and that most scouts get their feet wet in the business as part-time talent spotters in a particular area or region.

OTHER QUALIFICATIONS

Professional franchises rarely hire scouts fresh out of college. They most often hire former players and coaches, but they also employ those who have proven their scouting abilities through work with and a recommendation from one of their scouts.

College students should prepare a strong résumé, embark on a networking campaign, follow up with employers, be willing to relocate, and accept work as an intern or associate scout to start their careers.

JOB OUTLOOK

A rather rosy picture has been painted by the BLS concerning the future for coaches and scouts, which it lumped together in its analysis. It reported that 242,900 coaches and scouts held jobs in 2010 and that the number was expected to increase by 29 percent from that point to 2020.

The huge contracts offered to professional athletes increases the importance of strong scouting. Only the most successful keep their jobs.

The slowdown in professional sports expansion has slowed the pace of hiring for scouts, but there remains some growth in the business. Scouts are being increasingly looked at for management positions within their organizations.

WORK ENVIRONMENT

The BLS also confirms that coaches and scouts often work irregular hours, including evenings, weekends, and holidays, and are sometimes exposed during games and practices to extreme weather conditions. It stresses, too, that travel is most often extensive.

High school, college, and advance scouts spend an inordinate amount of time on the road. The often get little sleep and must eat on the run. Some spend half their time or more every year traveling. Those who could not embrace such a lifestyle should shy away from a scouting career.

Scouts not only work sporting events to evaluate athletes but also communicate with family members, coaches, and other associates of athletes to determine future success. Their jobs take them beyond the playing fields.

ADVANCEMENT

Only those who succeed in identifying and correctly evaluating high school and college athletes advance in the industry. Successful scouts can be given territories they prefer in which to scout or become advance scouts if that is more to their liking. Promotions into management positions and raises in pay are typical rewards for successful scouts. The ultimate goal for many scouts is to become a general manager of a professional organization.

GLOSSARY

advance scout A scout sent to a game of a future opponent to analyze a team to help his own team prepare to play that opponent.

amateur An individual who is not paid for his or her work in an activity or sport.

athletics director Head of a high school or college athletics department.

bird dogging Finding prospects, usually as a volunteer, to help an established scout and further a career.

bonus Money given up front to a prospect upon signing a contract.

free agent An athlete free to market his services to any team.

general manager The person in a professional sports organization making final decisions on player procurement.

graduate assistant A young college coach working on his master's degree and trying to further his career as a coach or scout.

internship Generally unpaid work to gain experience in a particular field.

interview A conversation between an employer and prospective employee in which the former asks questions of the latter to determine if the latter should be hired.

NCAA The National Collegiate Athletic Association, the primary governing body of college sports.

prep High school.

professional Individual who is paid to work.

prospect Any player in a sport being considered by scouts.

recruiting The job of a college coach seeking to convince particular athletes to accept a scholarship to his school.

reference A person whose name and contact information are provided by a job seeker to speak well of the job seeker to potential employers.

relocation Leaving home to take a job elsewhere.

résumé Brief written account of past academic and work achievements used to convince employers to hire a prospective employee.

scholarship Tuition offered by athletics departments to talented athletes in an attempt to lure them to their school.

scouting report A thorough evaluation of a prospect written by a scout and presented to his employer.

undergraduate Any college student who has not yet earned a degree.

FOR MORE INFORMATION

Major League Baseball (MLB)
245 Park Avenue
New York, NY 10167
(212) 931-7800
Web site: http://mlb.mlb.com/home
MLB is the home of thirty franchises with job sites online
   whose individual scouting departments can provide further information about employment opportunities.

Major League Baseball Scouting Bureau
3500 Porsche Way, Suite 100
Ontario, CA 91764
(909) 980-1881
Web site: http://mlb.mlb.com/mlb/official_info/about_mlb/
   scouting_overview.jsp
This is the parent organization of all MLB scouts. Its site
   gives thorough information about the job of scouting
   and provides contact information for prospective scouts.

Major League Soccer (MLS)
420 Fifth Avenue, 7th Floor
New York, NY 10018
(212) 450-1200
Web site: http://www.mlssoccer.com
The MLS features nineteen clubs in the United States and
   Canada. These teams offer some scouting opportunities.

National Collegiate Athletic Association (NCAA)
700 West Washington Street
P.O. Box 6222
Indianapolis, IN 46206-6222
(317) 917-6222
Web site: http://www.ncaa.org
This governing body provides resources, news, and information about college sports. Those seeking coaching
   opportunities should contact the athletics departments
   at individual schools.

National Football League (NFL)
280 Park Avenue, 15th Floor
New York, NY 10017
(212) 450-2000
Web site: http://www.nfl.com
The NFL houses thirty-two franchises around the country.
   Their job sites are online, and their scouting departments can be reached individually for possible openings
   and more information.

National Hockey League (NHL)
1185 Avenue of the Americas, 15th Floor
New York, NY 10036
(212) 789-2000
Web site: http://www.nhl.com
The NHL boasts thirty franchises in the United States and
   Canada. Those curious about scouting possibilities for
   any of those organizations should seek out their job sites
   or contact their scouting departments directly.

Sports Financial Advisors Association
10645 North Tatum Boulevard, Suite 200-608
Phoenix, AZ 85028
(602) 820-2220

Web site: http://www.sportsfinancial.org
This organization is dedicated to providing financial advice
    and aid to a wide array of professionals in the sports
    industry.

Sports Management Worldwide
1100 NW Glisan Street, Suite 2B
Portland, OR 97209
(888) 952-4368
Web site: http://www.sportsmanagementworldwide.com
This group offers online courses for prospective general
    managers and scouts interested in baseball, basketball,
    football, hockey, and soccer.

WEB SITES

Due to the changing nature of Internet links, Rosen
Publishing has developed an online list of Web sites related
to the subject of this book. This site is updated regularly.
Please use this link to access the list:

http://www.rosenlinks.com/GCSI/Scout

Coakley, Jay. *Sports in Society: Issues and Controversies.* New York, NY: McGraw-Hill, 2008.

Crevin, Matt. *Get in the Game: The Ultimate Game Plan for Transition to College to Career.* Voice of the Box Productions, 2012. E-book.

DeSensi, Joy Theresa, and Danny Rosenberg. *Ethics and Morality in Sport Management.* Morgantown, WV: Fitness Information Technology, 2010.

Devantier, Alecia T., and Carol A. Turkington. *Extraordinary Jobs in Sports.* New York, NY: Facts On File, 2006.

Ferguson Publishing. *Ferguson's Careers in Focus: Sports.* 4th ed. New York, NY: Facts On File, 2008.

Field, Shelly. *Career Opportunities in the Sports Industry.* New York, NY: Checkmark Books, 2010.

Field, Shelly. *Managing Your Career in the Sports Industry.* New York, NY: Checkmark Books, 2008.

Freedman, Jeri. *Dream Jobs in Sports Management and Administration.* New York, NY: Rosen Publishing, 2013.

Greenwald, John. *Field Guides to Finding a New Career: Sports Industry.* New York, NY: Ferguson Publishing, 2010.

Heitzmann, Ray. *Careers for Sports Nuts & Other Athletic Types.* New York, NY: McGraw-Hill, 2004.

Hopwood, Maria, James Skinner, and Paul Kitchin. *Sport Public Relations and Communication.* Burlington, MA: Elsevier, 2010.

Howell, Brian. *Sports* (Inside the Industry). San Francisco, CA: Essential Library, 2011.

Hunter, Nick. *Money in Sports* (Ethics of Sports). Chicago, IL: Heinemann Library, 2012.

Lindstrom, Erick, and Erika K. Arroyo. *Sports* (Discovering Careers). New York, NY: Facts On File, 2010.

McKinney, Anne. *Real Resumes for Sports Industry Jobs.* Fayetteville, NC: Prep Publishing, 2004.

McLeish, Ewan. *Sports Industry* (A Closer Look: Global Industries). New York, NY: Rosen Publishing, 2011.

Pratt, Ancel R. *Jewels of the Game—How to Get a Job Working in Sports.* Lulu.com, 2011.

Reeves, Diana Lindsey. *Career Ideas for Kids Who Like Sports.* New York, NY: Checkmark Books, 2007.

Sandoval, Jim, and Bill Nowlin, eds. *Can He Play? A Look at Baseball Scouts and Their Profession.* Society for American Baseball Research, 2011. Kindle ed.

Schaaf, Phil. *Sports, Inc.: 100 Years of Sports Business.* Amherst, NY: Prometheus Books, 2003.

Schultz, Christian Dahl. *Ferguson Career Launcher: Professional Sports Organizations.* New York, NY: Ferguson Publishing, 2011.

Trenberth, Linda, and David Hassan, eds. *Managing Sports Business: An Introduction.* London, England: Routledge, 2011.

Wells, Michelle, Andy Kreutzer, and Jim Kahler. *A Career in Sports: Advice from Sports Business Leaders.* Livonia, MI: M. Wells Enterprises, 2010.

BIBLIOGRAPHY

BaseballHall.org. "Diamond Mines." Retrieved August 27, 2013 (http://scouts.baseballhall.org/history).

Baseball Reference. "Henry Powell." Retrieved August 8, 2013 (http://www.baseball-reference.com/minors/player.cgi?id=powell001hen).

Boles, Brian. "Opportunity of a Life-Time at the MLB Scouting Bureau's 'Scout School' (Scout Development Program)." Center for Neighborhood Enterprise, October 18, 2011. Retrieved August 22, 2013 (http://www.cneonline.org/wp-content/uploads/2012/09/MR_11_10-18_B_Boles.pdf).

Dragseth, P. J., ed. *Eye for Talent: Interviews with Veteran Baseball Scouts.* Jefferson, NC: McFarland & Company, Inc., 2010.

Gabriel, Greg. "You Want to Be a Scout? The Job May Seem Glamorous, but It's Far from Easy." *National Football Post*, July 19, 2010. Retrieved August 9, 2013 (http://www.nationalfootballpost.com/You-want-to-be-a-scout.html).

Juhl, Michael (Professional Scout, St. Louis Cardinals). Interview with the author, July 26, 2013.

Kerrane, Kevin. *Dollar Sign on the Muscle.* New York, NY: Simon & Schuster, 1984.

Koebler, Jason. "High School Sports Participation Increases for 22nd Straight Year." *U.S. News*, September 2, 2011. Retrieved August 27, 2013 (http://www.usnews.com/education/blogs/high-school-notes/2011/09/02/high-school-sports-participation-increases-for-22nd-straight-year).

Mason, Tyler. "Twins Sign First-Round Draft Pick Kohl Stewart." Fox Sports North, June 19, 2013. Retrieved August 25, 2013 (http://www.foxsportsnorth.com/mlb/minnesota-twins/story/Twins-sign-first-round-draft-pick-Kohl-S?blockID=913401).

McAdam, Sean. "Scouts Must Dig Deeper Than Tools." ESPN SportsZone. Retrieved August 26, 2013 (http://www.hsbaseballweb.com/pro-scouting/scouts_dig_deep.htm).

NBA.com. "Erik Spoelstra Biography." Retrieved August 27, 2013 (http://www.nba.com/coachfile/Erik_Spoelstra).

NBA.com. "Mike Brown Biography." Retrieved August 27, 2013 (http://www.nba.com/coachfile/mike_brown).

NHL.com. "2013 NHL Draft Selections." Retrieved August 25, 2013 (http://www.nhl.com/ice/news.htm?id=675878).

Pro Football Reference. "CNE Salutes: Youth Coach Chosen for MLB Scout Development Program." 1995 Draft Listing. Retrieved August 8, 2013 (http://www.pro-football-reference.com/years/1995/draft.htm).

Putula, Pete (Baseball Operations Assistant, Houston Astros). Interview with the author, July 23, 2013.

Ringolsby, Tracy. "Future GMs Might Come from Scouting Ranks." Fox Sports, March 23, 2010. Retrieved August 28, 2013 (http://msn.foxsports.com/mlb/story/Future-general-managers-could-come-from-baseball-scouting-ranks-032210).

Schneider, Russell. *The Cleveland Indians Encyclopedia.* 3rd ed. Champaign, IL: Sports Publishing LLC.

Shonka, Dan (General Manager and National Scout, Ourlads Scouting Service). Interview with the author, July 30, 2013.

Slater, Matt (Director, Player Personnel, St. Louis Cardinals). Interview with the author, July 24, 2013.

Sports Management Worldwide. "Basketball GM and Scouting Course." Retrieved August 23, 2013 (http://www.sportsmanagementworldwide.com/courses/basketball-scouting/faq).

Stack, Kyle. "The NBA's Only Female Scout." *Slam Magazine*, July 3, 2010. Retrieved August 27, 2013 (http://www.slamonline.com/online/nba/2010/07/the-nbas-only-female-scout).

Stoller, Gary. "San Francisco Giants Scout Loves Life of Travel." *USA Today*, July 23, 2013. Retrieved August 16, 2013 (http://www.usatoday.com/story/travel/2013/07/22/san-francisco-giants-scout-loves-his-life-of-travel-/2575495).

Vitello, Paul. "Edith Houghton, Rare Woman Among Baseball Scouts, Dies at 100." *New York Times*, February 15, 2013. Retrieved August 27, 2013 (http://www.nytimes.com/2013/02/16/sports/baseball/edith-houghton-rarity-as-baseball-scout-dies-at-100.html).

Wong, Glenn M. *The Comprehensive Guide to Careers in Sports.* Sudbury, MA: Jones & Bartlett, 2008.

Zipfel, Pat. "Traveling Man: Rockets Advance Scout Pat Zipfel Chronicles His Life on the Road." Houston Rockets, January 20, 2009. Retrieved August 14, 2013 (http://www.nba.com/rockets/news/An_Inside_Look_at_the_Life_of_-295509-34.html).

INDEX

ABOUT THE AUTHOR

Marty Gitlin is an educational book writer and sports writer based in Cleveland, Ohio. He has had more than seventy-five books published, many in the sports realm. During his twenty-five years as a newspaper sportswriter, he won more than forty-five awards, including first place for general excellence for the Associated Press for his coverage of the 1995 World Series. That organization also selected him as one of the top four feature writers in Ohio in 2001. Gitlin covered the Cleveland Browns for CBSSports.com from 2009 to 2012 before landing work as a fantasy football and baseball writer for that Web site in 2013.

PHOTO CREDITS

Cover, p. 1 ARENA Creative/Shutterstock.com; pp.4–5 Chuck Solomon/Sports Illustrated/Getty Images; p. 10 Dave Sandford/National Hockey League/Getty Images; p.14 Robert Beck/Sports Illustrated/Getty Images; pp. 16–17 Michael Zagaris/Getty Images; pp. 18–19 Jared Wickerham/Getty Images; p. 21 Al Bello/Getty Images; p. 25 Copyright 2007 NBAE. Photo by Dave Egan/NBAE/Getty Images; pp. 28, 37, 69, 73 © Sports Management Worldwide; p. 33 © University of South Carolina Athletics; 40–41, 45, 59 © AP Images; pp. 42, 70–71 MLB Scouting Bureau; p. 48 Angels Baseball; p. 52 Michael G. Smith/Shutterstock.com; p. 55 Copyright 2009 NBAE. Photo by Dave Einsel/NBAE/Getty Images; p. 57 Helen H. Richardson/Denver Post/Getty Images; p. 63 Mike Stobe/Getty Images; pp. 66–67 Purdue University Athletics Communications; pp. 78–79 JGI/Jamie Grill/Blend Images/Getty Images; p. 85 The Washington Post/Getty Images; pp. 88–89 Copyright 2008 NBAE. Photo by Ned Dishman/NBAE/Getty Images; p. 90 Dave Reginek/Getty Images: p. 92 Otto Greule Jr./Getty Images; p. 95 Brace Hemmelgarn/Getty Images; p. 97 Jonathan Daniel/Getty Images; interior design elements (graph) © iStockphoto.com/hudiemm, (stripes) Lost & Taken; pp. 8, 24, 36, 51, 65, 83, 99, 101, 107, 109, 115, 117, 120, 122, 125 © iStockphoto.com unless otherwise noted. From top left ultramarinfoto, Kayann, VIPDesignUSA, plherrera, cb34inc, yai112, Jimmy Anderson, dbrskinner, dswebb, Gannet77, Sergieiev/Shutterstock.com; gzaleckas, choja, cscredon, peepo.

Designer: Brian Garvey; Editor: Kathy Kuhtz Campbell;
Photo Researcher: Marty Levick